FOUND!

ROMAN BRITAIN

Moira Butterfield

FRANKLIN WATTS
LONDON • SYDNEY

Franklin Watts
First published in Great Britain in 2017 by The Watts Publishing Group

Credits
Series Editor: John C. Miles
Series Designer: Richard Jewitt
Picture researcher: Diana Morris
Picture Credits: Anteromite/Shutterstock: 1 bg, 2-3 bg, 30-31 bg, 33 bg. Simon Balson/Alamy: front cover main, 21l. Anthony Brown/Dreamstime: 12-13 bg. Colchester Museums: 5l. David Cole/Alamy: 1c, 13tr. Cosma/Shutterstock: back cover br. coxy58/Shutterstock: 15tr. Cranach/Shutterstock: front cover t. c paul fell/Shutterstock: 23tr. Dave G Houser/Getty Images: 17tr. LuFeeTheBear/Shutterstock: front cover bg. National Trust PL/Alamy: 25tr. Jaime Pharr/Shutterstock: 19tr. Photogenès: 18-19 c. Portable Antiquities Scheme/CC Wikimedia: 29tr. Alex Ramsay/Alamy: 29l. Michael Rosskothen/Shutterstock: 5tr. Patrick Rowney/Dreamstime: 24-25 bg. Adam Sorrell/Museum of London: 21tr. Rasiel Suarez/CC Wikimedia Commons: back cover tl. udra11/Shutterstock: front cver bg c. Steve Vidler/Alamy: 16-17. Wessex Archaeology: 7t, 7c, 8-9, 9tr, 11tr, 22-23, 26-27bg, 27tr. WHA/Alamy: 11l, 15l.

HB ISBN 978 1 4451 5298 1
PB ISBN 978 1 4451 5299 8

Printed in China

Franklin Watts
An imprint of
Hachette Children's Group
Part of The Watts Publishing Group
Carmelite House
50 Victoria Embankment
London EC4Y 0DZ

An Hachette UK Company
www.hachette.co.uk

www.franklinwatts.co.uk

CONTENTS

Here come the Romans – Gravestone of Longinus 4

Dressing like a Roman – Channel Tunnel hare 6

A Roman town – Durnovaria 8

Roman gods – The Uley Mercury 10

A magical swim – Bath Roman baths 12

Meet the army – Ribchester Helmet 14

Fight! – Bignor mosaic 16

A letter from the north – Vindolanda Tablets 18

I'm in charge – Head of Hadrian 20

Buying the best – Kingsmead Bowl 22

A luxury home – Chedworth 24

Roman burials – Boscombe Down 26

A buried hoard – Mildenhall Treasure 28

Glossary 30

Further information and Timeline 31

Index 32

GRAVESTONE OF LONGINUS

Nearly 2,000 years ago, in CE 43, the Roman army arrived to conquer Britain, which they called Britannia. The invading soldiers fought for the Roman Empire, ruled by an emperor based in Rome. They gradually conquered the Celtic tribes who controlled southern Britain. We can tell how brutal the fighting was from the tombstone of a conquering Roman called Longinus. He is shown trampling a Celt under his horse.

Around CE 49
Soon after the Romans arrived

DATE FOUND: FIRST FOUND IN 1928 BY WORKMEN.

PLACE FOUND: COLCHESTER, ESSEX.

In 1928 workmen were building a garage in Colchester when they uncovered a carved stone fragment. It turned out to be the tombstone of a Roman soldier called Longinus Sdapeze. Longinus's face was missing and experts wondered if it had been deliberately damaged by Celtic rebels who fought back against the Romans. But 70 years later archaeologists uncovered other parts of the stone, including the face, and pieced it together.

The Roman army arrived by ship, like the ones shown in this imaginary picture. They first landed on the coast of Kent or Sussex. We're not sure where exactly.

When Longinus lived in Colchester it was called Camulodunum. It was once a stronghold of the Celts but the Romans took it over and built an army fort there. Longinus was in charge of some troops based at the fort. He died aged 40 but we don't know how.

The fiercest Celtic warriors fought naked except for a sword belt. The Celt on the tombstone is shown this way. He has long hair and a moustache and beard, unlike the Roman invaders, who were short-haired and clean-shaven.

Longinus came from what we now call Bulgaria. Longinus's fellow soldiers would have organised his funeral and his gravestone, since he died a long way from his home and family.

How would you have felt if you were a Celt seeing the Romans arrive?

Dressing like a Roman
CHANNEL TUNNEL HARE

After many years of fighting, southern Britain eventually became peaceful under Roman rule. More and more Roman people arrive to live and work in the new province. We can tell what they wore by looking at statues and wall paintings, and from precious finds such as this beautiful hare-shaped brooch found in Kent.

Between
CE 100-300

DATE FOUND:
2000, DURING AN ARCHAEOLOGICAL DIG.

PLACE FOUND:
SPRINGHEAD, KENT.

Before the Channel Tunnel Rail Link was built, archaeologists discovered lots of Roman objects at Springhead in Kent, along the route. Springhead was a Roman religious centre because of its water springs. The Romans thought that springs were connected to gods and goddesses. They threw objects, such as the brooch, into the waters to please the gods.

A Roman brooch is called a *fibula*. It works like a big safety pin for fixing clothing in place, usually on the shoulders. The hare brooch was made of copper with blue and green enamel decoration.

Roman men wore short tunics, but in Britain they added woolly leggings and a cloak pinned on with a brooch. They would only put on a toga if they were going to a smart occasion.

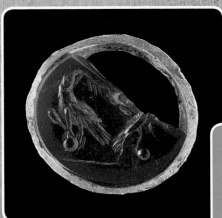

This is the bezel (top part) of a Roman ring found at Springhead. It is called an intaglio, and it shows a carving of two eagles. The eagle was a symbol of Rome.

'Romano-British' is the name we give to the people who lived in Britain under Roman rule. Over time locals intermarried with Romans and began to copy the way the newcomers behaved. They began to wear Roman-style clothing and jewellery.

Roman women wore an undertunic and a long overtunic called a *stola*. In cold weather they added a shawl called a *palla*. They wore jewellery, such as bracelets, rings, earrings and necklaces.

How similar to Roman jewellery is the jewellery we wear today?

A Roman town
DURNOVARIA

The Romans built Britain's first towns. In fact, some of today's towns were founded in Roman times and have Roman remains hidden beneath them. For instance, anyone walking through Dorchester in Dorset is actually stepping on the remains of the Roman town of Durnovaria. Archaeologists have found buildings and belongings on two town sites – one site under a hospital and one site under a shopping street.

CE 100-300

DATE FOUND:
COUNTY HOSPITAL SITE EXCAVATED 2000–2001. CHARLES STREET EXCAVATED 2011.

PLACE FOUND:
DORCHESTER, DORSET.

Archaeologists took a look at the two Dorchester sites before modern building work was started. At the hospital site they found the remains of wooden buildings, ovens and rubbish thrown out by the Romans. At Charles Street (the picture shown here) they found more houses, along with pottery, coins and even board game counters. Their discoveries showed that Roman Durnovaria was a busy place where people lived, worked and played.

This beautiful hairpin was found at the hospital site. It was carved from animal bone, and shows the Roman god Cupid. It would have been an expensive luxury to own. Someone in Durnovaria would have used it to put up her hair the smart Roman way!

Durnovaria had shops, baths workshops and government buildings. It had a defensive wall around it and roads connecting it to other parts of Roman Britannia.

In the area of town shown here, there were once Roman homes with mosaic floors. One had a walkway of columns running around a courtyard. It might have surrounded a peaceful garden away from the bustle of the town.

It's thought that the people of Durnovaria were mostly Romano-British – local people who began living the Roman way. We know they ate Roman-style food because the remains of olive oil storage jars were found in the Charles Street homes. The jars would have been shipped all the way from Spain.

What similarities can you think of between Roman Durnovaria and a modern town that you know?

Roman gods
THE ULEY MERCURY

The Romans believed in lots of gods and goddesses. They built temples dedicated to them and made them offerings to keep them happy. Temples were dotted around southern Britain, including one at Uley, Gloucestershire, dedicated to the god Mercury. The head of his temple statue was rediscovered in the 1970s.

CE **100s**
Date when the statue was made

DATE FOUND:
THE TEMPLE WAS FOUND IN 1976, THEN EXCAVATED.

PLACE FOUND:
ULEY, GLOUCESTERSHIRE.

In 1976 workmen laying a water pipe stumbled on the buried remains of Uley's Roman temple. When archaeologists took a closer look they found Mercury's head carefully buried in the ground, and fragments of his statue around the site. There was Roman accommodation and shops around the temple, too, for visitors who came to worship Mercury. But why was the statue deliberately smashed up in late Roman times?

Romans believed that Mercury was the youngest son of Jupiter, the King of the gods. He was smart, fun and good at trickery. He could use his magical winged sandals, staff and hat to fly fast, and these would probably have been on his statue when it was complete. It would have been around 2 m tall.

This is an aedicule, a little portable Roman shrine made of lead. It was found in the town of Dorchester (see p. 8) and it shows the goddess Minerva (see p. 12). Romans put mini shrines like this in their own homes, to worship every day.

Excavations showed that Uley was a shrine long before the Romans arrived. Local Britons probably worshipped their nature gods and goddesses there. The Romans often built their own temples on local religious sites.

Towards the end of Roman times, Christianity arrived in Britain. At first it was illegal and punished with imprisonment. But when the Roman Emperor Constantine became a Christian, it was accepted. Bible pictures made on copper have turned up at Uley, evidence that Christians lived here in the 300s. It's possible that they smashed up the statue and buried the head, superstitious of its power.

Are there religious buildings near where you live? Some may be decorated with religious statues in the same way as Roman temples.

A magical swim
BATH ROMAN BATHS

Many Romans went to public baths, which were rather like modern spas. One of the grandest bath complexes in Britain was in the town of Aquae Sulis – now called Bath – where the pool waters came from a natural hot spring that was thought to be sacred and magically healing.

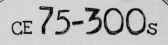

CE 75-300s

The years when the baths were used

PLACE FOUND:
BATH,
SOMERSET.

DATE FOUND:
REDISCOVERED IN
1775 BY BUILDERS.

In 1727, a large bronze head from a Roman statue was discovered by workmen digging a sewer trench in Bath. More Roman remains began turning up and then, in 1775, builders found the remains of some magnificent Roman public baths, fed by an underground hot spring. The Romans believed that the spirit of the goddess Minerva dwelled in the Aquae Sulis hot spring. The bronze head (top right) probably belonged to her statue.

Visitors to the baths could relax in a series of heated rooms. They could take a plunge in a cold pool or swim in the large, hot bathing pool. Slaves would rub them with olive oil and gently scrape it off their skin to cleanse them.

The hot spring bubbled up in a sacred pool, thought to be a magical portal where people could communicate with the goddess Minerva. Visitors threw treasures in, hoping to please her and bring themselves good luck. Roman coins and pieces of jewellery have been found in the drains below the baths.

The head of Minerva, shown here, was gilded (covered with gold). It would have been on an impressive, larger-than-life statue.

A mysterious tin mask was discovered at the baths. It might have been used by priests in ceremonies held to honour Minerva.

Visitors sometimes threw curses into the sacred pool. The curses were pleas to the goddess to inflict revenge on someone for a wrongdoing. They were inscribed on small sheets of lead.

If you were going to throw something into the sacred pool to please the goddess, what would you choose?

Meet the army
RIBCHESTER HELMET

The Roman army were stationed in forts around the country. In around CE 120 someone based at a fort in Ribchester, Lancashire, packed some military possessions in a wooden box, put them away for safekeeping and never retrieved them. They were rediscovered by a little boy over 1,600 years later.

Between CE 100-200
The date when the mask was packed away

DATE FOUND: 1796, BY A BOY PLAYING BEHIND HIS HOUSE.

PLACE FOUND: RIBCHESTER, LANCASHIRE.

In 1796 a clog maker's son was playing on waste ground behind his house when he found lots of rusty metal. It turned out to be a hoard of equipment from the nearby Roman fort. The hoard included the fabulous, bronze Ribchester Helmet. It would once have been worn by a cavalry soldier performing in a riding demonstration, perhaps for a VIP visiting his fort.

Helmets like this were worn in mock battle and riding sports demonstrations called *hippika gymnasia*. They usually took place on a parade ground outside a fort, and they were a good opportunity for soldiers to show off their skills.

The Ribchester Helmet is one of only three similar helmets found in Britain. The father of the boy who found it sold it to a local collector, but we don't know how much he got for it. In 2010 one of the other helmets sold for £2.3 million!

Cavalry horsemen wore elaborate costumes for sports displays and parades, but they wouldn't have worn elaborate headgear like the Ribchester Helmet in battle.

The Roman army was organised into groups of soldiers called legions, each with its own commanders, and foot soldiers called legionaries. Legionaries were Roman citizens who came from Rome, whereas cavalrymen were usually soldiers born elsewhere in the Roman Empire. We know that around the time the helmet was used, a unit of cavalry from Spain was based at Ribchester.

What type of Roman object would you like to discover?

Fight!
BIGNOR MOSAIC

Large Roman towns and army bases in Britain had arenas called amphitheatres, where people went to see gladiators fight to the death or watched them pitted against wild animals. A mosaic discovered in the remains of a Roman country home shows a picture of gladiators training under the eye of their instructor.

Late
CE **200s**
– early
CE **300s**
Date of mosaics

DATE FOUND:
1811, BY A FARMER PLOUGHING IN A FIELD.

PLACE FOUND:
BIGNOR, WEST SUSSEX.

In 1811 farmer George Tupper struck a piece of stone with his plough. It turned out to be a fountain belonging to a large Roman villa – a luxury country home with fine floor mosaics. Once they were fully uncovered, crowds flocked to see some of the best mosaic pictures ever found in Britain.

The mosaic shows two gladiators training. Their instructor looks on, carrying a wooden staff that he can use to separate them. There were different kinds of gladiators, armed and dressed in different ways. The gladiators in the mosaic are a retiarius and a secutor.

A big amphitheatre has been uncovered at Chester, once the Roman town of Deva Victrix. The crowds left behind bones from their arena snacks, entry tokens and even souvenir pots with pictures of gladiators on them.

The gladiators in the mosaic have wings, perhaps because the artist imagined them as mythical beings. The figure of a goddess (not shown) is above them in the mosaic, so perhaps they are entertaining her. We can't tell, but the mosaic owner would no doubt have understood the picture.

The retiarius is fighting with a three-pronged trident. The secutor is carrying a curved shield and a short sword called a gladius. The mosaic tells a story over several sections, like a cartoon. Another section of the mosaic shows the secutor defeating the wounded retiarius.

If you were a gladiator, would you rather have a sword or a trident?

A letter from the north
VINDOLANDA TABLETS

The Romans never conquered Scotland. Instead they set up a frontier zone of forts and lookout posts across northern England. It was a way to control the movement of people and goods, and keep an eye on the Picts – tribes who lived in Scotland and were prone to cattle-stealing and smuggling. The forts were manned by Roman soldiers. They wrote and received letters that survived in the ground for 2,000 years.

CE 97-103
Time period of the letter writing

DATE FOUND: 1973, BY AN ARCHAEOLOGIST.

PLACE FOUND: BARDON MILL, NORTHUMBERLAND.

Archaeologist Robin Birley found wood fragments in a waterlogged Roman rubbish heap on the site of a fort called Vindolanda. When the pieces were peeled apart they revealed Latin handwriting, the earliest handwriting ever found in Britain. Hundreds of wooden tablet pieces were eventually discovered, telling stories of ordinary people living at the fort.

The tablets were made from slivers of wood about the size of a postcard. Once written, they were scored and folded in half, with the address on the outside. They were tied shut with binding cord.

The remains of Vindolanda are shown here. It was in an isolated place, and the Roman soldiers who manned the fort would have been very far from their European homes.

Some of the writing was about official business, such as lists of food supplies ordered for the troops. Some were letters written to the soldiers themselves. From one of the letters we can tell that a lucky soldier was sent new underpants and socks! These would have been very welcome in chilly northern Britain.

The soldiers would have met local Romano-British people, and some might even have had families with local women. We know that some of the soldiers didn't think much of the locals, though. On one tablet the writer used an insulting nickname – the *Brittunculi* – meaning 'little Britons'.

In one of the letters, a lady called Claudia Severa invited her friend Sulpicia Lepidina to a birthday party, and hoped very much that she would come. The two friends were both wives of Romans serving near the fort.

When was the last time you wrote a letter to someone?

I'm in charge
HEAD OF HADRIAN

Roman emperors sent top officials to govern Britain for them. They rarely visited themselves, but in CE 122 the Emperor Hadrian arrived. Londinium (London) was smartened up for his visit and his bronze statue may have been put on show. Over 1,700 years later the statue's head was pulled out of the River Thames.

Possibly
CE **122**

The date Hadrian visited

DATE FOUND: 1834, PULLED OUT OF THE RIVER.

PLACE FOUND: THE RIVER THAMES, UNDER LONDON BRIDGE, LONDON.

When a new London Bridge was being built in 1834, workers fished out the head of the Emperor's statue from the river. The Romans founded Londinium, and by the time Hadrian visited the town it was Britain's most important port and government centre. His larger-than-life bronze statue was either put up to commemorate his visit or placed in a temple dedicated to him. Emperors were worshipped as gods after they died.

This picture is a reconstruction of how Londinium might have looked in Roman times.

In Londinium, Hadrian would have found a big public square called the Forum, lined with shops and temples. On one side of the square there was an impressive three-storey government building called the Basilica.

Hadrian was born in Spain and became emperor of Rome because of his military successes. He was an efficient and military-minded emperor. He travelled around his empire, strengthening its borders against enemies. In Britain he ordered the building of a wall across northern England to protect Britannia from the Picts (see p. 18). It was named Hadrian's Wall.

Although people in Britain rarely saw emperors, they would know what they looked like from statues, busts and coins. The Emperor Hadrian was the first emperor to grow a beard, and when people saw it on his statues it started a new fashion for beards across the Roman Empire.

If you had your own statue where would you like it to be?

Buying the best
KINGSMEAD BOWL

ce 120-145

If they could afford it, Romano-British people liked to buy luxury goods, such as the best dining bowls and glassware, to impress their friends. The most stylish and expensive examples came from abroad, like this decorated bowl found at the site of a Roman farm in Berkshire.

DATE FOUND: FINDS STARTED TURNING UP ON THE SITE IN 2003.

PLACE FOUND: KINGSMEAD QUARRY, HORTON, BERKSHIRE.

Archaeologists investigating parts of Kingsmead Quarry found the remains of a Romano-British farm. The people who lived there probably sold their crops at nearby Pontibus, now called Staines. They were wealthy enough to buy a top-notch, decorated dining bowl to use on special occasions.

The fragments of the bowl have been pieced together to show a hunting scene of stags and lions. It is a type of bright-red pottery called Samian ware. The potter stamped his mark on the bottom so we know it was made in Gaul (now France).

The farm owners probably had slaves to cook their meals. If visitors came they might have tried to impress by serving up unusual meats, such as roast wild boar, along with sauces flavoured with expensive imported spices. They would no doubt have used their best Samian ware, too.

Goods were brought to British ports by merchant ships from all over the Roman Empire. This Tunisian mosaic shows a merchant ship, perhaps laden with spices, olive oil or wine for eager Roman customers.

Poor Romano-British people would not have owned expensive dishes or eaten luxury food. They would have lived on broth with some vegetables or meat bones thrown in, served in cheap pottery. If they were lucky, they might find some wild herbs to flavour their plain food.

The Romans introduced many new foods to Britain, including the herbs thyme and rosemary, and vegetables, such as onions, cabbage, celery, garlic, leeks and peas. They brought apples, cherries and domestic chickens, too.

Which foods that the Romans brought to Britain do you eat?

A luxury home
CHEDWORTH

Most Romano-British people would have lived in small wooden homes rather like shacks with thatched roofs, but the richest families had stone-built country houses called villas. A few of these luxury country retreats have been rediscovered, including Chedworth Villa in Gloucestershire.

CE **360-380**
The date when the villa was at its grandest

DATE FOUND: 1964, BY A GAMEKEEPER DIGGING IN A WOOD.

PLACE FOUND: CHEDWORTH, GLOUCESTERSHIRE.

When a local gamekeeper found mystery buried remains, further digging soon revealed fine mosaic floors – evidence that wealthy people once lived in a luxury Roman-style home on the site. It turned out to be one of the best-preserved Roman villas so far found in Britain.

The villa had everything for comfortable living. Its luxuries included a bathhouse and an underfloor heating system called a hypocaust. It even had its own farm for producing food.

The villa was near the important Roman town of Corinium, now called Cirencester. It might have belonged to an important local family connected to the town, but we don't know for sure.

The Romans brought edible snails over to Britain, fattening them up with milk to eat as a delicacy. A few descendants of these rare Roman snails still live around Chedworth Villa. They are twice as big as ordinary snails.

Slaves would have had to work hard to keep Chedworth Villa warm in the chilly British winter. They had to keep a fire constantly burning to warm air that circulated under the floors in the hypocaust.

All the work at the villa would have been done by slaves belonging to the family. Roman slaves were either captive war prisoners or they were born into slavery. Any child born to a slave automatically belonged to the slave-owner.

Chedworth had mosaic floors and wall paintings. What do you have on the floors and walls of your home?

Roman burials
BOSCOMBE DOWN

We can tell something about how Romano-British people lived and what they believed by looking at ways they were buried. Five cemeteries found near Boscombe Down in Wiltshire turned out to contain the remains of around 300 people who lived and worked locally in Roman times.

CE **200-400**
Date span of all the burials

DATE FOUND: THE STONE COFFIN WAS FOUND IN 2007.

PLACE FOUND: BOSCOMBE DOWN, WILTSHIRE.

Archaeologists have been digging around Boscombe Down since the late 1990s. Since that time they have found the graves of many people who once lived in a Roman farming community. Most of the graves had wooden coffins, but in 2007 the archaeologists unearthed their most unusual find – a stone coffin dating to around CE 220. When they lifted the lid they had a big surprise …

Inside the stone coffin lay the body of a woman carrying the body of a child in her arms. The chemical conditions inside the coffin meant that the remains were very well preserved. Even the lady's deer-skin slippers and the child's calf-skin shoes had survived.

Most of the people buried at Boscombe Down would have believed in the Roman underworld, a shadowy kingdom where the dead were thought to live. The dead journeyed across a river to the underworld, rowed by a ferryman called Charon. Some of the people in the cemetery had coins buried with them, probably to pay him.

We don't know how the woman and her child died, but we do know that life would have been short for most of the people buried at Boscombe Down. Only about a quarter of them lived over the age of 35.

The lady's relatives had prepared her for a journey to the next world. She wore clothes and jewellery and had a pretty, shiny pot that probably contained a drink for her to have on her journey.

Have Roman belongings been found near where you live? Find out at your local museum.

A buried hoard
MILDENHALL TREASURE

CE 300s

DATE FOUND:
1942, BY A
PLOUGHMAN.

By the CE 400s Rome was facing attack from many enemies, and the Roman army left Britain to defend other parts of the Roman Empire. Life became much more difficult and dangerous for those left behind. Someone may have buried a glittering silver treasure around this time, to keep it safe. We call it the Mildenhall Treasure.

PLACE FOUND:
MILDENHALL,
SUFFOLK.

In 1942 a ploughman and a farmer uncovered a hidden stash of Roman silverware. The farmer kept the finds a secret for years. When they were revealed, some people suggested that such fine treasures might have been stolen from Italy during the Second World War (1939–45). Later finds around Britain proved that fine silver pieces such as these were owned by Romano-British people.

The biggest piece in the hoard is the Mildenhall Dish, shown here. It measures just over 60 cm wide. The middle of the dish shows the head of Neptune, god of the sea.

Some Roman hoards are mainly coins. In 2010 a metal detectorist found 52,503 coins hidden beneath a field in Frome, Somerset. It was the biggest Roman coin hoard ever found in Britain.

Eventually Roman Britain was overrun by Saxon invaders. Romano-British people might have fled, been killed, captured as slaves or lived alongside the raiders. Perhaps all of these things happened. We do know that the Saxons lived very differently from the Romans and life changed a great deal.

Hoards such as the Mildenhall Treasure may have been buried because, by the late 300s, Saxon raiders were attacking southern Britain from areas we now call Germany and Denmark. Other parts of Roman Britain were suffering attacks from Irish and Scottish tribes.

If you had to hide your best possessions where would you hide them? Would you bury them?

Glossary

aedicule   A small, portable Roman shrine.

amphitheatre   A large arena surrounded by tiers of seats and used for Roman entertainment, such as gladiator fights.

archaeologist   Someone who studies bones and the remains from human activity in the past.

basilica   The most important government building in a Roman town.

cavalry   Soldiers who fought on horseback. Today the cavalry fight in armoured vehicles.

Celtic   The name we give to the tribes who lived in Britain before the Romans invaded.

clog maker   Someone who makes wooden shoes, called clogs.

conquer   To take over, usually by force.

fort   A building designed to be used to look out for and defend against attacks.

forum   A public square in the centre of a Roman town used as a marketplace or for other business.

founded   Started.

frontier   A line or border that separates two countries.

hippika gymnasia   Mock battles and sporting contests held between Roman cavalry soldiers at their fort.

inscribe   To carve words into something.

intermarry   When people from different races, classes or religions marry.

Latin   The language of ancient Rome and the official language of the Roman Empire.

legion   A company of Roman soldiers, rather like a modern regiment.

legionary   A Roman foot soldier.

merchant   Someone who buys and sells goods.

mosaic   A picture made up of tiny coloured squares.

parade   A formal gathering of troops for inspection or display, which often takes place on a parade ground.

portal   A doorway or entrance.

province   A Roman-governed territory outside of Italy, such as Britain.

Roman Empire   An area of Europe, North Africa and the Middle East ruled by the Romans. Rome was founded around 750 BCE and the Empire reached its greatest extent in Western Europe around CE 395.

sacred   Something connected to a god or a religion, such as an object or a place.

Saxons   People from the areas we now call Denmark and Germany. They began to raid Roman Britain in the late 300s, and they eventually settled there.

scored   A mark scratched into a surface.

shrine   A religious site where people come to worship a god (or gods).

spring   A place where water wells up from underground.

symbol   A mark, letter or drawing that stands for something else.

toga   A robe worn by Roman men on smart occasions or when they were on official business.

tunic   A loose garment that covered the body to the knees.

underworld   A shadowy kingdom where the Roman dead were thought to live.

Further Information

WEBLINKS

www.youtube.com/watch?v=D-VmbxpEFAA

An imagined day in the life of a 10 year-old in Roman Britain, produced by the BBC.

www.britishmuseum.org/learning/schools_and_teachers/resources/cultures/ancient_rome.aspx

Access the Roman resources of the British Museum, for children.

www.tribunesandtriumphs.org/roman-life/ancient-roman-recipes.htm

Try out some Roman recipes, including a Roman form of burgers and some delicious honey and nut concoctions.

Note to parents and teachers: Every effort has been made by the Publishers to ensure that the websites in this book are suitable for children, that they are of the highest educational value, and that they contain no inappropriate or offensive material. However, because of the nature of the Internet, it is impossible to guarantee that the contents of these sites will not be altered. We strongly advise that Internet access is supervised by a responsible adult.

TIMELINE

CE 43 The Roman army invaded southern Britain as ordered by Emperor Claudius.

CE 49 Camulodunum (now called Colchester) was founded. It was briefly Britain's capital.

CE 61 Some British Celtic tribes rebelled, led by queen Boudicca, but they were defeated.

CE 75 The Roman baths of Aquae Sulis were founded around this date.

CE 97–103 The time period when the Vindolanda Tablets were written.

CE 122 Emperor Hadrian visited Britain and ordered the building of Hadrian's Wall.

CE 211/212 Britain was divided into two provinces (government areas). Londinium (London) was the capital of the south. Eboracum (York) was the capital of the north.

CE 220 The stone coffin found near Boscombe Down was buried around this time.

CE 306 Constantine became Emperor of the Roman Empire.

CE 314 Constantine ordered an end to the persecution of Christians.

CE 367 Attacks on the frontiers of Roman Britain were becoming a serious problem.

CE 410 The Roman army left Britain and the Romano-British people were left to try to defend themselves from attacks and invasion by the Saxons.

Index

aedicule 11
amphitheatres 16, 17
Aquae Sulis (see Bath)

Bardon Mill 18–19
basilica 21
Bath 12–13
baths 9, 12–13, 25
Berkshire 22–23
Bignor 16–17
Boscombe Down 26–27
brooch 6–7

Camulodunum 5
Celts 4–5
cemeteries 26–27
Channel Tunnel 6
Charon 27
Chedworth 24–25
Christianity 11
clothing 6–7, 19, 26, 27
coffins 26–27
coins 8, 13, 21, 27, 29
Colchester 4
Constantine 11
copper 6, 11

Dorchester 8–9, 11
Dorset 8–9
Durnovaria 8–9

farmers/farming 16, 22–23, 25, 28
fibula 6–7
food 9, 19, 22–23, 25
forts 5, 14, 18–19
forum 21
Frome 29

Gauls 22
gladiators 16–17
Gloucestershire 10–11, 24–25
goddesses/gods, Roman 6, 9, 10–11, 12–13, 20, 28
  Cupid 9
  Jupiter 10
  Mercury 10–11
  Minerva 11, 12, 13
  Neptune 28

Hadrian 20–21
Hadrian's Wall 21
hairstyles 5, 9
hoards 14–15, 28–29
homes 8–9, 16–17, 24–25
hypocausts 25

jewellery 6–7, 13, 27

Kent 5, 6–7

Lancashire 14–15
legionaries/legions 15
London 20–21
London Bridge 20
Longinius 4–5

Mildenhall Treasure 28–29
mosaics 9, 16–17, 23, 24, 25

Northumberland 18–19

olive oil 9, 12, 23

palla 7
Picts 18, 21

pottery 8, 17, 22–23, 27

religion 6, 10–11
Ribchester Helmet 14–15
River Thames 20–21
Roman army 4–5, 14–15, 16, 28
Roman Empire 4, 15, 21, 23, 28
Romano–British 7, 9, 19, 22, 23, 24, 26, 29

Samian ware 22–23
Saxons 29
Scotland 18
silver 28–29
slaves 12, 23, 25, 29
Somerset 12–13, 29
Spain 9, 15, 21
spas 12–13
Springhead 6–7
springs 6, 12–13
stola 7
Suffolk 28–29
Sussex 5, 16–17

temples 10–11, 20, 21
togas 7
tombstones 4–5
tridents 17

Uley Mercury 10–11
underworld 28

Vindolanda Tablets 18–19

Wiltshire 26–27

These are the lists of contents for titles in the FOUND! series:

STONE AGE

The first people: The Happisburgh footprints • Extra-special skull: Swanscombe Woman • Modern man + magic: Goat's Hole Cave • Butchered bones: Gough's Cave • Ice Age artists: Creswell Caves • A long-lost lake: Star Carr • Underwater treasure: Bouldner Cliff • Home cooking on the farm: Windmill Hill pots • Top axes: Langdale axe factory • Trash tells a story: Skara Brae • Tribes of fur and feather: Tomb of the Eagles • Glossary • Timeline • Websites • Index

BRONZE AGE

Bringer of Metal: Amesbury Archer • Clues to solve: Boscombe burials • Making metal: Great Orme • Mystery messages: Gardom's Edge stones • Buried treasures: Mold Cape • Bronze Age clothes: Whitehorse Hill cist • Pottery detective work: Newbald food pot • Under us now: Heathrow Airport • A buried beast: Kingsmead Quarry • Time to travel: Peterborough boat fleet • Watery world: Must Farm • Water treasure: Loch Glashan • For a fine warrior: Moel Hebog shield • Glossary • Timeline • Websites • Index

ROMAN BRITAIN

Here come the Romans: Gravestone of Longinus • Dressing like a Roman: Channel Tunnel hare • A Roman town: Durnovaria (Dorchester) • Roman gods: The Uley Mercury • A magical swim: Bath Roman baths • Meet the army: Ribchester Helmet • Fight!: Bignor mosaic • A letter from the north: Vindolanda Tablets • I'm in Charge: Head of Hadrian • Buying the best: Kingsmead Bowl • A luxury home: Chedworth • Roman burials: Boscombe Down • A buried hoard: Mildenhall Treasure • Glossary • Timeline • Websites • Index

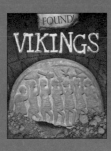

VIKINGS

Attack!: Lindisfarne Priory Stone • Here to stay: Repton Great Army • Caught by enemies: The Weymouth Massacre • Farming Vikings: Jarlshof • A busy workplace: Coppergate • Viking style: Jorvik clothing • A Viking wise woman: The Lady of Peel • A Viking parliament: Tynwald Hill • A Viking leader: Ardnamurchan ship burial • Hidden treasure: Silverdale Hoard • Reading the runes: Maeshowe • Viking pictures: St Paul's Rune Stone • A new god: Horn of Ulf • Glossary • Timeline • Websites • Index

Also in the series: